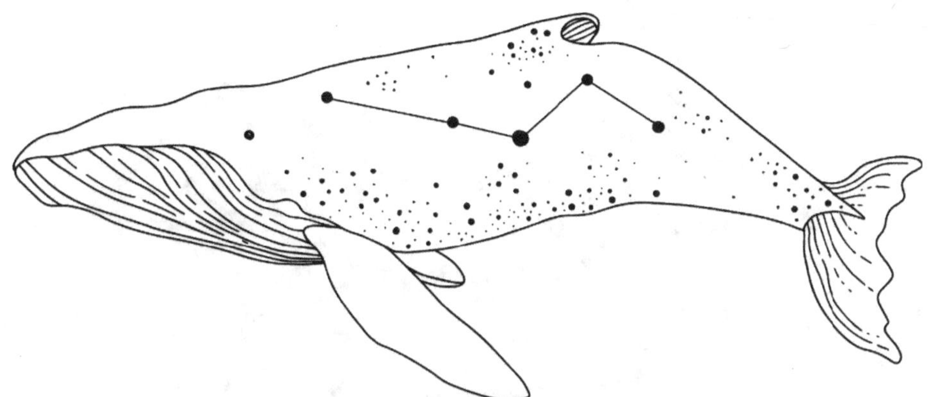

THIS BOOK

BELONGS TO

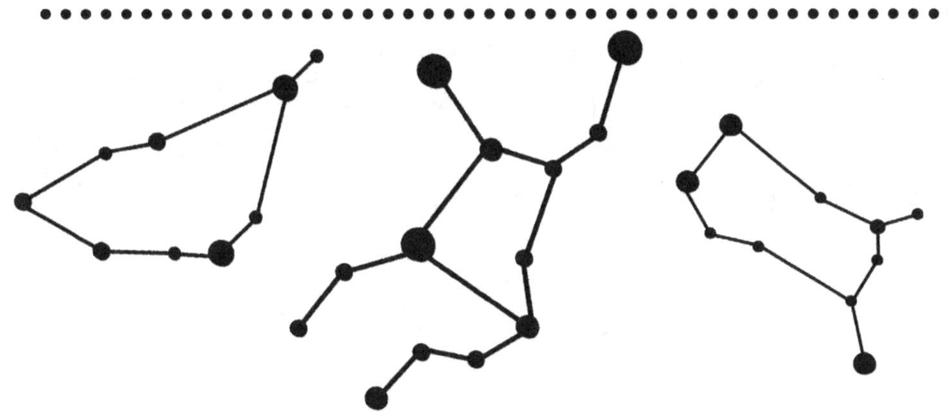

Aries

An Aries is anyone born between March 21 and April 19.

Friend Lists

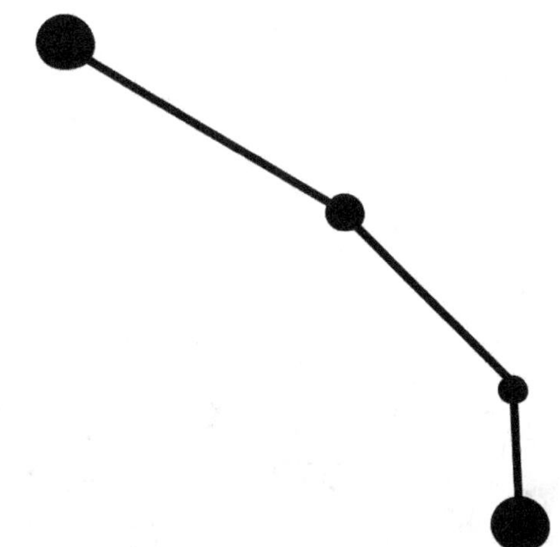

Aries is full of optimism and unbridled hope, making them highly generous and eager to help those in need, just so they can put a smile on people's faces.

Zodiac element : Fire

What signs are compatible with Aries?

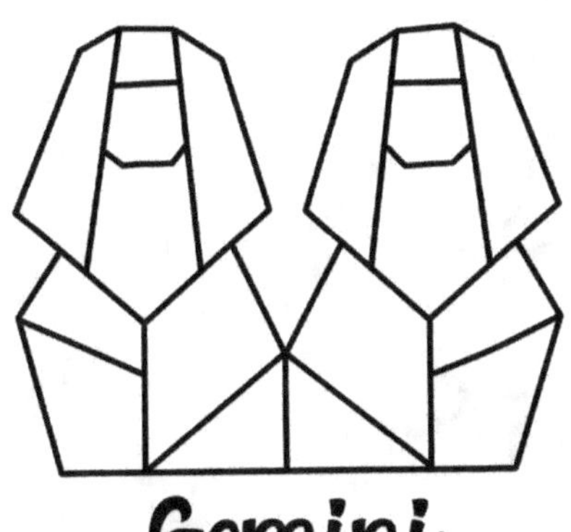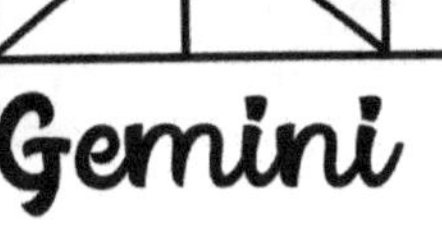

Gemini

Sagittarius

Leo

Aquarius

Taurus

The Taurus sign represents people born between April 20 and May 20.

Friend Lists

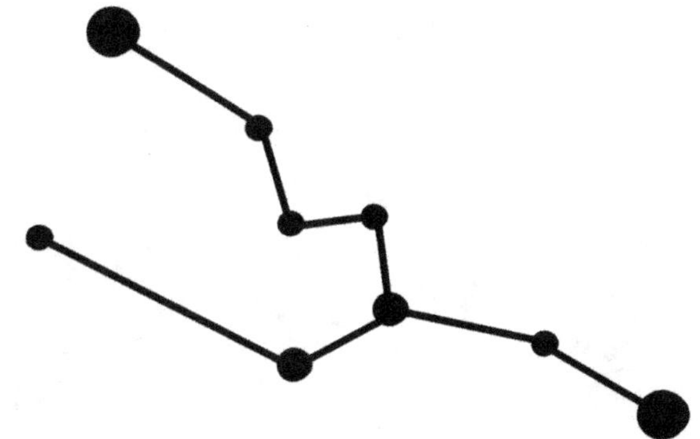

Taurus is an earth sign. Taureans, like the bull that represents them, are known to be intelligent, dependable, hardworking, dedicated, and stubborn.

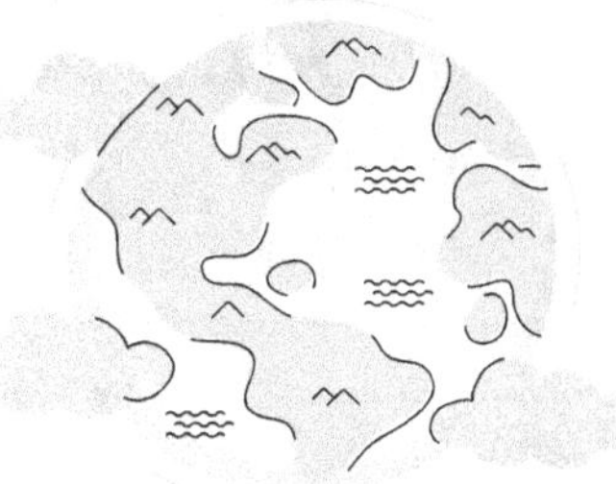

Zodiac element : EARTH

What signs are compatible with Taurus?

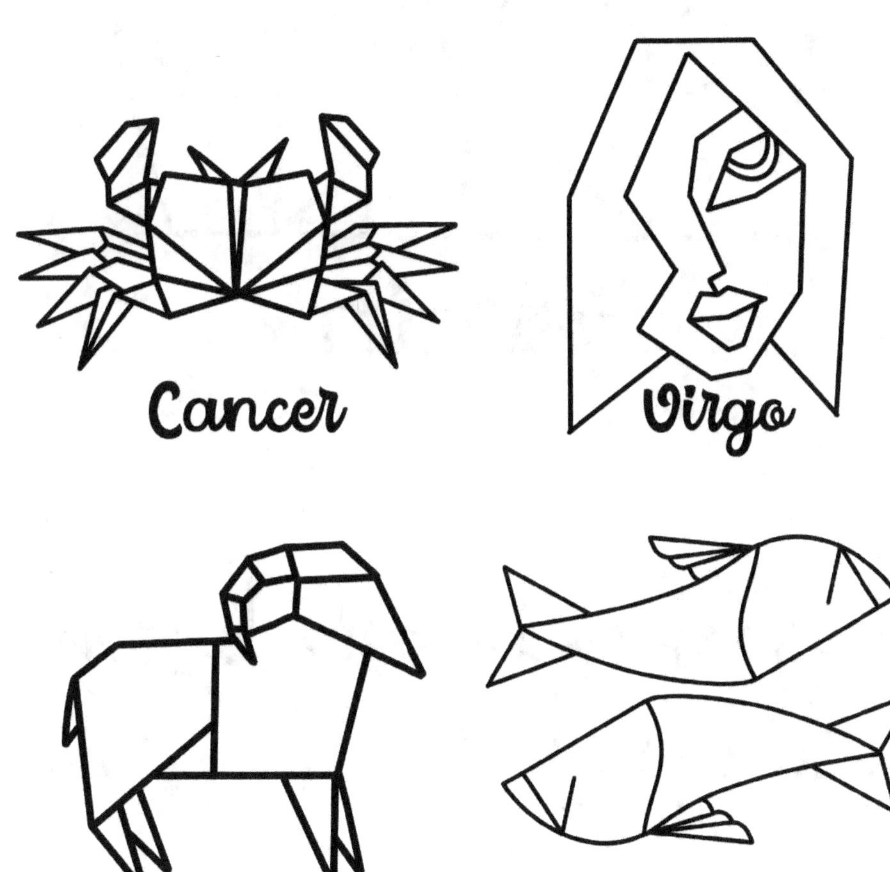

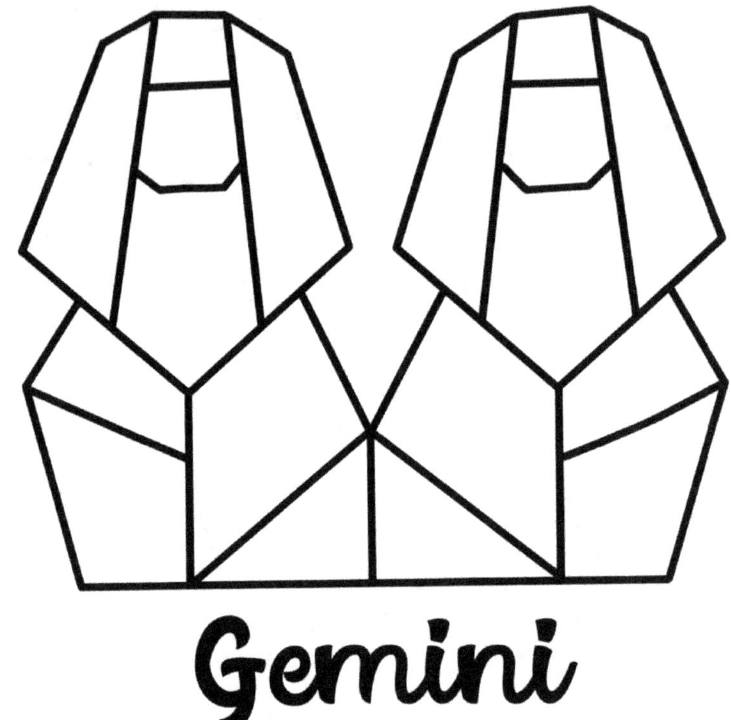

Gemini

Geminis are born between May 22 and June 22.

Friend Lists

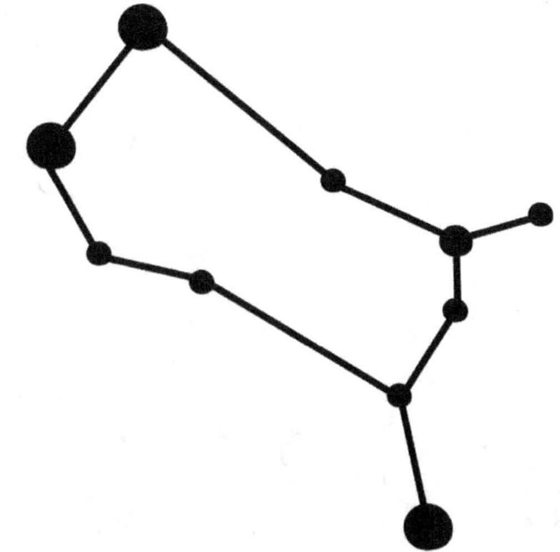

Playful and intellectually curious, Gemini is constantly juggling a variety of passions, hobbies, careers, and friend groups.

Zodiac element : AIR

What signs are compatible with Gemini?

Capricorn

Leo

Libra

Aquarius

Cancer

Those who are born from approximately June 21 to July 22 are born under Cancer.

Friend Lists

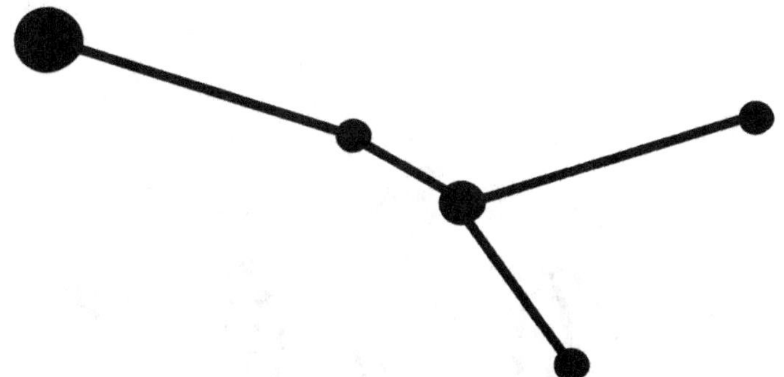

Cancer can be one of the most challenging zodiac signs to get to know. They are very emotional and sensitive, and care deeply.

Zodiac element : WATER

What signs are compatible with Cancer?

Leo

Leos, born July 23 – August 22

Friend Lists

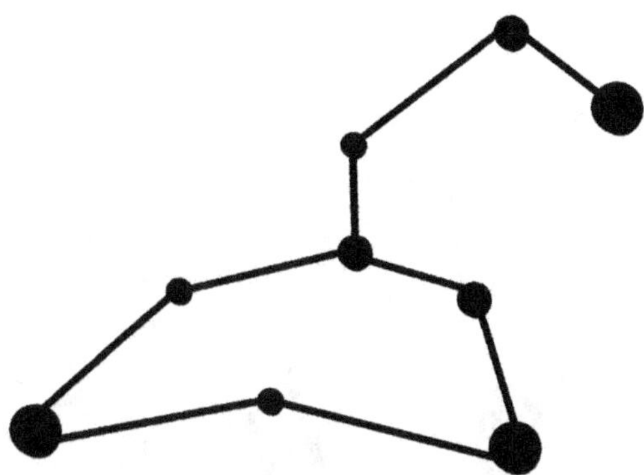

People born under the sign of Leo are natural born leaders. They are dramatic, creative, self-confident, dominant and extremely difficult to resist, able to achieve anything they want to in any area of life they commit to.

Zodiac element : FIRE

What signs are compatible with Leo?

Capricorn

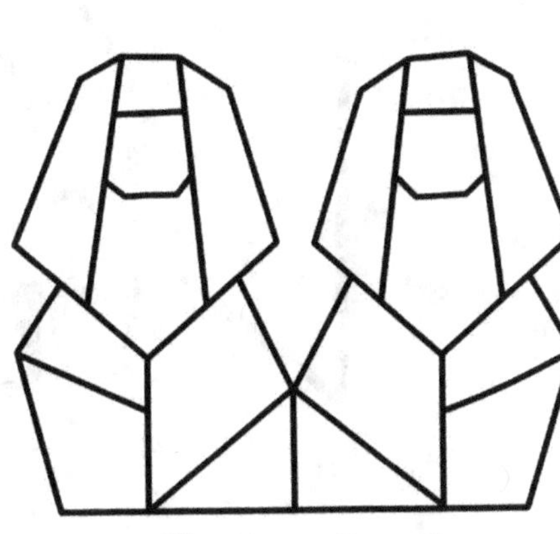

Gemini

Libra

Sagittarius

Virgos are born between August 23 and September 22

Friend Lists

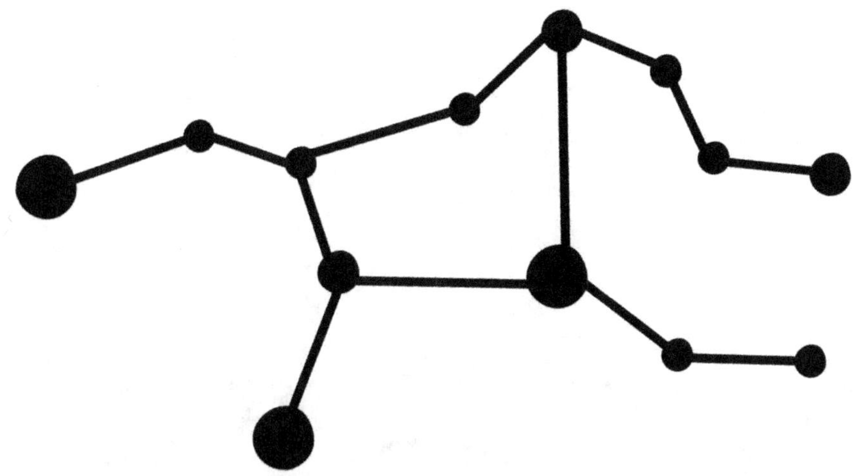

Virgo Zodiac Sign. Smart, sophisticated, and kind, Virgo gets the job done without complaining. Virgos are amazing friends, always there to lend a hand

Zodiac element : EARTH

What signs are compatible with Virgo?

Taurus

Cancer

Capricorn

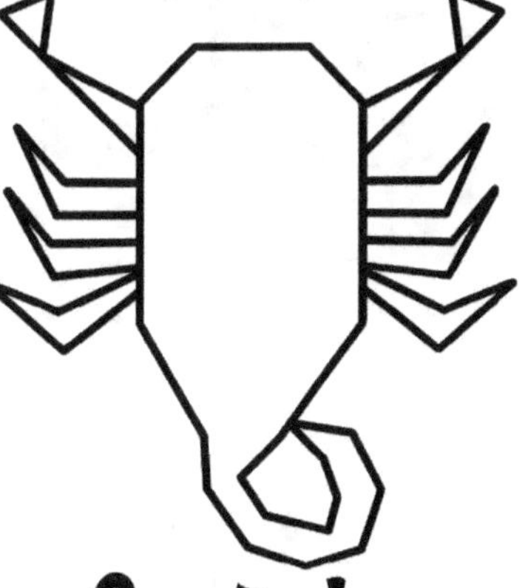

Scorpio

Libra

Librans are born between September 23 and October 22

Friend Lists

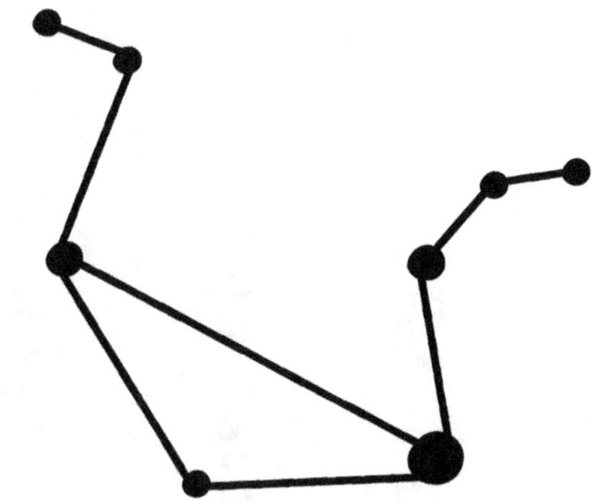

Libras are known for being charming, beautiful, and well-balanced. They thrive on making things orderly and aesthetically pleasing. They also crave balance

Zodiac element : AIR

Who are Libras most compatible with?

Leo

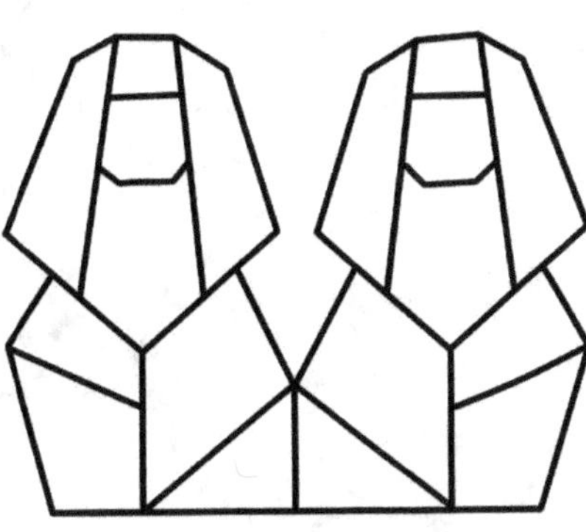

Gemini

Sagittarius

Aquarius

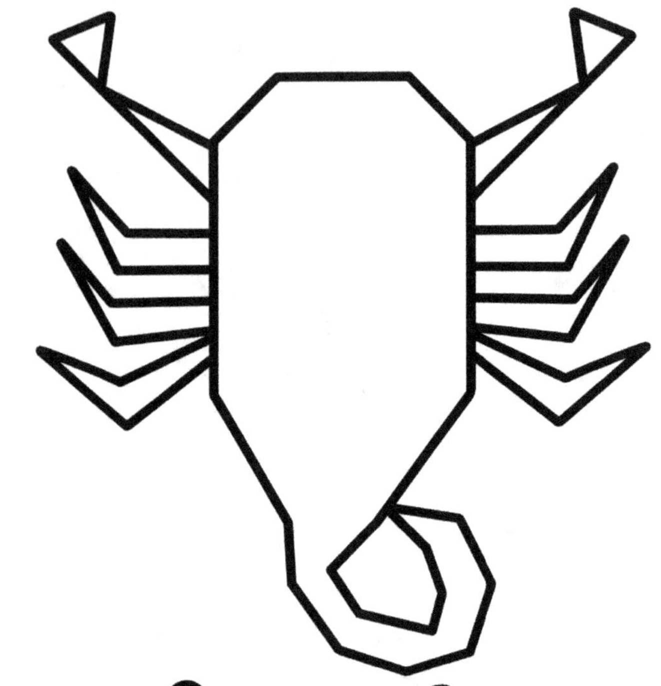

Scorpio

Scorpio dates in astrology are typically from October 23 to November 21

Friend Lists

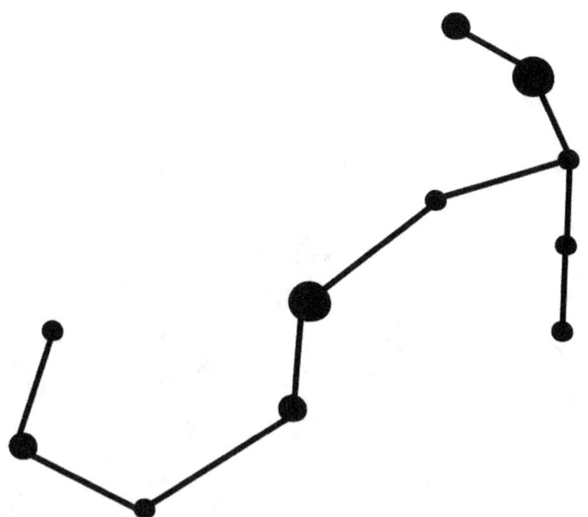

Scorpios simply know what they want and aren't afraid to work hard and play the long game to get it. They never show their cards and their enigmatic nature is what makes them so seductive and beguiling

Zodiac element : WATER

What signs are compatible with Scorpio?

Virgo

Cancer

Capricorn

Pisces

Sagittarius

Sagittarius is a sign of the zodiac that represents people born between November 23rd and December 21st

Friend Lists

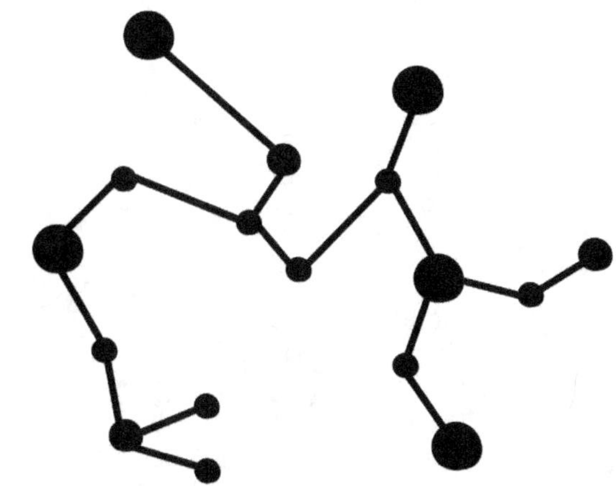

Sagittarians are optimistic, lovers of freedom, hilarious, fair-minded, honest and intellectual. They are spontaneous and fun, usually with a lot of friends, and are perhaps the best conversationalists in the zodiac

Zodiac element : FIRE

What signs are compatible with Sagittarius?

Aries

Leo

Libra

Aquarius

Capricorn

Those born between December 22 and January 19.

Friend Lists

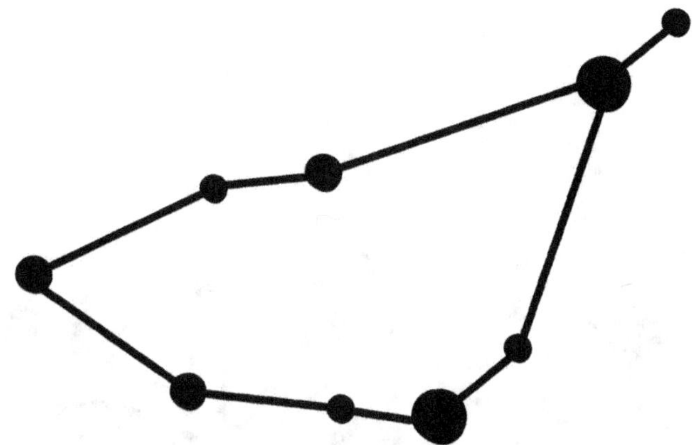

Capricorns are the ultimate worker bees. They're ambitious, organized, practical, goal-oriented, and they don't mind the hustle. They also love making their own rules.

Zodiac element : EARTH

What signs are compatible with Capricorn?

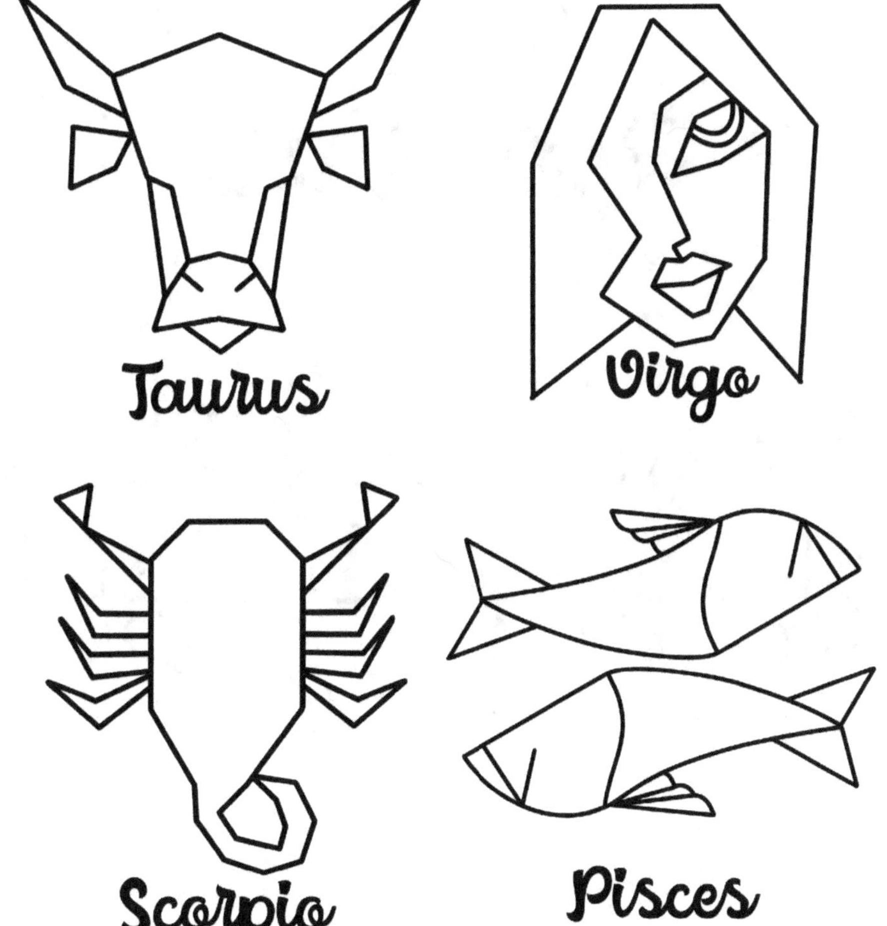

Aquarius

Those born between January 20 and February 18.

Friend Lists

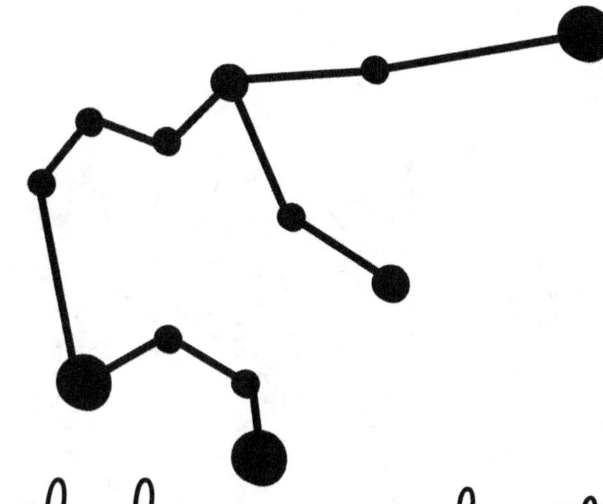

People born under the Aquarius sign are said to be progressive, independent, intelligent, unique, and idealistic.

Zodiac element : AIR

What signs are compatible with Aquarius?

Aries

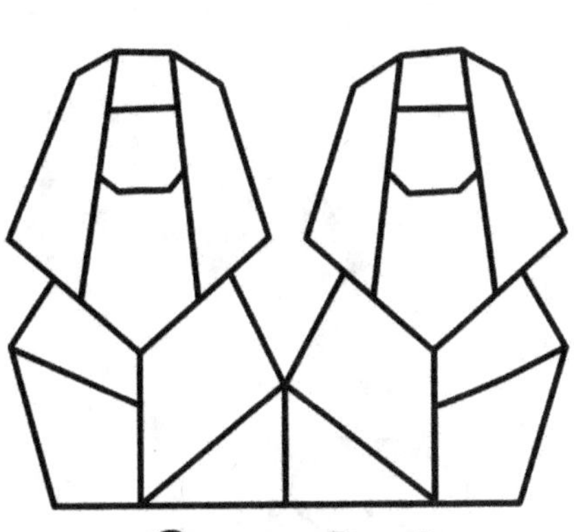

Gemini

Libra

Sagittarius

Pisces

Pisces are born between February 20th and March 20th,

Friend Lists

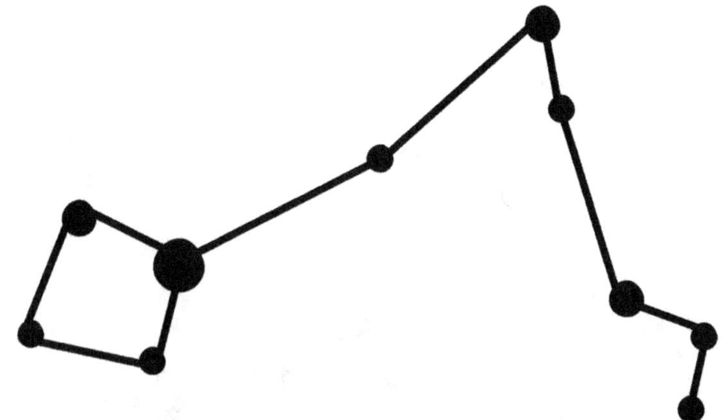

Fish personalities are known to be one of the most empathetic signs of the zodiac and will do whatever they can to make sure the people around them are happy. They are also artistic gifted

Zodiac element : WATER

What signs are compatible with Pisces?

Thank You